Virtual Reality in Astrophysics

Discovering and Observing the Celestial Bodies

Table of Contents

Chapter 1. Introduction

Dive into a celestial universe like never before with our special report on "Virtual Reality in Astrophysics: Discovering and Observing Celestial Bodies." This thrilling overview is designed for everyone from seasoned astrophysicists to starstruck novices, illuminating the revolutionary intertwining of virtual reality technology and space exploration. Forget about jargon-heavy technical reports: our guide takes a down-to-earth approach, unraveling the complex advancements in a manner that's both engaging and accessible. So, strap on your virtual reality headset and let's embark on a galactic journey that will leave you starry-eyed – an expedition that's literally out of this world, and only a report purchase away!

Chapter 2. Journey into Celestial Realities: The Marriage of VR and Astrophysics

A bountiful wealth of knowledge exists within the celestial sphere, fascinating humans for millennia, from our basic comprehension of the cosmos to today's technologically advanced studies. This has given rise to the integration of technology into our pursuit of understanding cosmic realities, the most prominent of which is the synergy of Virtual Reality (VR) and Astrophysics. The canvas is immense, but let's try to explore the cosmic intricacies with the lens of VR and the science of astrophysics.

2.1. Embracing the Cosmos: An Introduction to Astrophysics

Astrophysics, a branch of space science dealing with the physical elements and attributes of celestial bodies and the phenomena that occur externally to the Earth's atmosphere, opens the door to an exploratory world beyond our confined terrestrial existence. Decoding the science behind star emissions, interpreting the rotation of a distant exoplanet, or ascertaining the life cycle of the nearest galaxy, astrophysics sheds light on all these aspects and beyond.

2.2. The Virtual Leap: Understanding VR

Virtual Reality (VR) is an interactive computer-generated experience that mimics the environment and allows one to step into a space mimicking real-life scenarios. Using VR headsets, this immersive technology plunges us into a powerful sensory experience, immersing all five senses in environments far removed from our own.

2.3. The Confluence: VR and Astrophysics

The marriage of VR and astrophysics is a revolutionary step technically, educationally, and experientially. It allows individuals to virtually participate in cosmic tours, traversing through celestial bodies, feeling the exhilaration of a supernova's formation, or appreciating the dance of a binary star system. Basic principles of physics, daunting mathematical equations, and space theories turn into visual stories, creating a vibrant, virtually real, interstellar experience.

2.4. Rendering Cosmos in VR: Science meets Imagination

The crucial component herein is 'Data Visualization.' Semantic and volumetric mapping of space data collected through telescopes, observatories, and satellites is channelized into VR platforms. The resulting high-dimensional cosmos is then rendered in VR through complex computer algorithms and artificial intelligence, creating a scientifically accurate, immersive simulation.

2.5. Interstellar Sojourn: VR Experiences in Astronomy

Many organizations and institutions have embraced VR technology to recreate celestial experiences. Tools like "Universe Sandbox," "Titans of Space," "Celestron SkyPortal," etc., allow users to visit distant nebulas, study the surface of Mars, or scale the whole universe at their pace. Educational institutions employ VR to explain complex astrophysics concepts interactively, aiding in learning and retention.

2.6. Future Possibilities: Pushing the Boundaries

Looking at the future, VR in astrophysics holds immense potential. The installation of advanced tools in space observatories could enhance real-time experiences, adding a new dimension to space study. Concepts such as time dilation, black holes, and space-time fabric often sound mind-bending. However, these phenomena's interpretation through VR platforms has the potential to make these science-fiction-like elements of our universe more comprehensible.

2.7. The Roadmap: Achieving the Reality

To actualize these scenarios, hurdles like seamless interoperation of different VR devices, resolving issues of cyber motion sickness, and improving VR content to handle voluminous space data needs to be addressed. Collaborative projects between VR developers and astrophysicists could propel this wild cosmic ride into the household reality.

Unquestionably, the journey into celestial realities ably supported by VR is potent with not just scientific possibilities, but also a chance to satiate our innate human curiosity for space exploration. As the technology advances, the cosmos, once restricted to a select few scientists, can be accessible to everyone, shaping a new frontier in astrophysics. Welcome to a realm where you're not just a spectator, but a part of this cosmic waltz!

Chapter 3. The Science Behind the Stars: A Primer on Astrophysics

The ability to look up to the night sky and marvel at the sparkling expanse of the cosmos is a universal human experience. Since time immemorial, long before the birth of telescopes and astronomy, human eyes have gazed upon the stars, forming constellations and stories from the patterns they observed. But today, we're beginning to step beyond mere observation and interpretation. Through tools like virtual reality and the continuously evolving field of astrophysics, we are probing deeper into the universe, understanding and visualizing the complexities of celestial bodies like never before.

3.1. The Basics of Astrophysics

Astrophysics, a branch of astronomy, studies the physical nature of stars and celestial bodies, using a combination of observational data and theoretical physics. It looks at phenomena like stellar evolution, galaxy formation, and cosmic microwave background radiation, interpreting these to create a comprehensive understanding of the universe.

To facilitate the comprehension of astronomical and physical phenomena, astrophysicists use a series of equations, most notably those from classical and quantum mechanics, electromagnetism, statistical physics, thermodynamics, and relativity.

3.2. Grasping at Light: Understanding the Electromagnetic Spectrum

Much of what we know about the universe comes from studying the light emitted by celestial bodies. Visible light does play a key role but digging deeper into the electromagnetic spectrum, we find that different frequencies or wavelengths of light, from radio waves to gamma rays, can tell us more about the universe.

The Sun, for example, emits light across all frequencies, although maximum intensity falls in the visible spectrum. However, astronomers might want to study certain phenomena, such as solar flares, more intensively in the X-ray or ultraviolet spectrum. Each segment of the spectral data provides unique information about temperature, composition, velocity, and other physical properties of celestial bodies.

3.3. The Life of a Star: Birth, Life, and Death

Stellar evolution is another core area that astrophysicists delve into. They trace the life cycles of stars from their births within dense clouds of gas and dust, called nebulae, to their deaths as white dwarfs, neutron stars, or black holes.

Stars spend most of their lives fusing hydrogen into helium in a phase called the main sequence. The Sun is a prime example of a main sequence star. Upon exhausting their hydrogen supply, stars expand into red giants, ultimately shedding their outer layers and leaving behind a hot core.

When massive stars exhaust their nuclear fuel, they undergo a supernova explosion, spewing out their outer layers into space. Depending on the original star's mass, different end-states are possible: white dwarfs for less massive stars, neutron stars for more massive, and black holes for the most massive.

3.4. Galaxies: Island Universes

Astrophysics also encompasses larger structures - galaxies, clusters of galaxies, and superclusters, sometimes collectively termed as the "cosmic web". Galaxies are vast collections of millions to trillions of stars, bound together by gravity. Our galaxy, the Milky Way, is a barred spiral galaxy housing an estimated 100 billion stars.

The study of galaxies and their interaction helps us decipher the overall structure and evolution of the universe. It's through such studies that we've been able to surmise the existence of dark matter and dark energy, invisible entities that significantly influence galactic structures and the universe's expansion.

3.5. Shedding Light on the Dark: Dark Matter and Dark Energy

Dark matter and Dark energy together constitute a staggering 95% of the universe, but we neither see nor fully understand them. They remain two of the greatest mysteries in astrophysics.

Dark matter emerges from observations of galaxies and clusters. These structures move in ways that cannot be explained by visible matter alone. Astrophysicists inferred the existence of an unseen form of matter that does not interact with light, hence 'dark'.

Dark energy, on the other hand, is tied to the expansion of the universe. Observations reveal that the universe's expansion is accelerating. It's theorized that a mysterious form of energy, permeating all of space, is driving this acceleration – we call this dark energy.

3.6. Tomorrow's Universe: The Future of Astrophysics

Astrophysics is at a very exciting juncture. As technology advances and we develop powerful tools like the James Webb Space Telescope, and sophisticated VR simulations, we are poised to uncover mysteries that have eluded us for so long. The origin of black holes, the mysterious components of dark matter, the true nature of dark energy, the search for extraterrestrial life - are all tantalizing quests that the future of astrophysics holds, promising deeper, richer understandings of our remarkable universe.

By understanding the basics of astrophysics as discussed in this section, we are better placed to appreciate the innovations in VR technology that have transformed our understanding of the stars, nebulae, galaxies, and the cosmos at large. Pushing the boundaries of human knowledge, we step closer to answering fundamental questions about our origins and our place in the cosmos. The journey is still in progress, and with virtual reality in astrophysics, everyone is welcome aboard.

Chapter 4. Virtual Reality 101: An Introduction and Its Potential

Discovering distant celestial bodies and perusing through intangible galaxies is now becoming a conceivable reality, thanks to virtual reality (VR). A technology that, until recently, was considered the preserve of science fiction, is now teaching us unparalleled lessons about the universe. By providing new ways to visualize and understand vast celestial data sets, VR in astrophysics is paving the way to new cosmic inquiries and examinations.

4.1. A Quick Rundown of Virtual Reality

Born from a fusion of imagination and technology, virtual reality has the unique ability to transport users to different settings or world, differing from the ordinary viewing experience on a screen. In simple terms, it is a computer-generated simulation or recreation of a real (or imagined) environment or situation. VR immerses the user by simulating as many senses as possible, such as vision and hearing.

To experience VR, one typically wears a VR headset or helmet. Upon donning the headset, your vision is filled with a digitally rendered world. Most devices also contain a tracking system, which follows the user's movements and adjusts the images accordingly, giving the sensation of being "inside" the virtual world.

4.2. Virtual Reality vs. Traditional Methods

Traditional methods of studying astrophysics often involve complex mathematical models, technical diagrams, and illustrations. While these methods have driven astronomical discovery for centuries, they can be hard to grasp for the layperson and even present significant challenges for scientists.

In comparison, VR facilitates an immersive, visual experience where celestial bodies can be examined in three-dimensional space. Users can interact with the modeled environments, enabling a more intuitive understanding of the subject matter. Virtual reality allows for immersion and scale that a flat image or model simply cannot provide - the vastness of the cosmos is suddenly palpable and personal.

4.3. Exploring the Potential of VR in Astrophysics

There's an exciting myriad of potential applications when it comes to VR technology's usage in the field of astrophysics.

Virtual Observatories: With VR, exploring the Universe doesn't require a colossal telescope or a clear night sky. Virtual observatories equipped with VR technology offer detailed renditions of the cosmos, allowing users to explore distant galaxies, nebulae, and planets.

Data Visualization: Astrophysics routinely suffers from floods of data, presenting a challenge to understand and represent comprehensively. VR could be instrumental in handling this data deluge. In a VR environment, data can be displayed spatially, intuitively aiding the interpretation and comprehension of complex patterns and relationships in astronomical data.

Public Outreach and Education: VR can inspire people, young and old, by providing a personal, relatable experience of the universe. It is an invaluable tool for education, making complex astrophysical concepts understandable and interesting to the simply curious, students, and aspiring astronomers.

4.4. The Future of Astrophysics With VR

Virtual Reality's integration into astrophysics is far from a complete journey. Though the initial demonstrations of this synergy have been promising, they represent just a glimpse into what might be achieved in the future.

Researchers are developing immersive environments that not only visualize data but also enable manipulation, offering hands-on experience with celestial bodies and formations. Someday, VR may simulate gravitational forces, allowing researchers to feel their way through phenomena like black holes!

As we steep ourselves further into the realm of VR, the potential and possibilities are charting a trajectory that takes us straight to the stars and beyond. With enough dedication, collaboration, and technological advancement, we might one day traverse distant galaxies and comprehend cosmic wisdoms, without ever leaving our earthly home.

Unquestionably, Virtual Reality has started redefining astrophysics, turning the indescribable into something experiential and providing us with a chance to truly touch the stars. Who knows, the amalgamation of VR and astrophysics may well end up being our time's greatest answer to the cosmos's oldest questions.

Despite the hurdles, the limitless potential of VR to revolutionize our understanding of the universe makes the pursuit entirely worthy. A future where anyone can discover the wonders of the cosmos is suddenly within our grasp – if we dare to reach for it.

Chapter 5. Visualizing the Universe: The Role of VR in Observing Space

From the ground, a telescope can only offer so much in terms of visualizing the cosmos. It is the technological marriage of astrophysics and virtual reality (VR) that has the potential to elevate this experience, providing humankind a means to visually explore and observe objects in space like never before.

5.1. Embracing the Virtual

In its essence, virtual reality is a simulated experience that can mirror the physical world or take users to completely new dimensions. This technology has made significant strides in many fields and is now setting its sights skyward. VR's immersive nature makes it an ideal tool for transforming vast and complex cosmological data into a relatable representation.

Researchers and developers are now leveraging the capabilities of VR to provide users with a first-hand exploration of the universe. Maps of the universe, constellations, and visuals of distant galaxies are all within reach of the VR user. From home, classroom, or lab, anyone can be transported to the observable edges of the universe. This unprecedented blend of scientific accuracy and immersive experience allows a new perspective on our positioning in the cosmic pattern.

5.2. Unwrapping the Cosmic Blueprint

Astro-visualization, the process of translating scientific data into graphical, cinematic formats, serves as the foundation for the creation of these VR environments. The data collected from various sources, such as the Hubble Space Telescope and the Chandra X-ray Observatory, includes information on celestial body positioning, movement, and composition. Processed through computer algorithms, this data is transformed into 3D visuals.

These visuals supplement textbooks and enrich didactic tools, thereby helping to bridge the gap between complex cosmic phenomena and traditional classroom teaching environments. This promotes easy comprehension and an increased interest in astrophysics' many mystifying facets.

5.3. The Interactive Cosmos

VR advances astrophysics further by allowing for an active investigation of celestial bodies. Users have the opportunity to virtually navigate spaces not accessible by physical probes or rovers, lending them the chance to interact with stars, planets, galaxies, and even phenomena like black holes and supernovae.

Astrophysicists and amateur astronomers alike can alter their viewpoint and perspective, simulate events, and even travel through space-time, fostering a palpable connection with the universe's capabilities.

5.4. VR and Space Missions

Space agencies worldwide are assessing VR's potential to improve mission success rates. VR can safely mimic environments for astronaut training, teaching spacewalk procedures, vehicle operation, and even preparing astronauts for the harsh realities of space travel. Its use extends to mission visualization, giving scientists a tool for exploring landing sites or navigating routes within the formidable environment of space.

In terms of remote exploration, rovers and probes outfitted with cameras transmit environmental data back to Earth. This data can be fed into VR systems, allowing researchers to explore extraterrestrial terrain visually.

5.5. The Future of VR in Astrophysics

While we have only scratched the surface of possibilities, VR's future in astrophysics conceivably shines bright. The next frontier is the enhancement of multi-sensory experiences, including the integration of haptic feedback to replicate the physical texture of celestial bodies.

The evolution of quantum computing holds the potential to handle increasingly complex astro-visualization, heightening the fidelity and realism of the VR cosmos. There is also the exciting prospect of using VR for collaborative space exploration where scientists worldwide can work together in a shared virtual realm.

However, achieving these milestones relies on resolving certain challenges — making VR more affordable and user-friendly, ensuring accurate data translation, improving resolution, and reducing motion sickness experienced by some users.

In conclusion, virtual reality could be the key that allows humankind a closer look at the cosmos. It holds immense potential for transforming our interaction with and understanding of the universe, it only remains for us to harness its full potential. Only at that milestone can we truly see the universe in a way that goes beyond our earthbound limitations.

Chapter 6. Experiential Learning in Astrophysics: Leveraging VR for Education

In recent years, the domain of astrophysics has been revolutionized by the advent of immersive technologies like Virtual Reality (VR). These advancements have been instrumental in bridging the gap between complex astrophysical concepts and learners, effectively transforming abstract theories into tangible, interactive experiences. In an academic landscape fraught with heavy textbooks and intricate equations, VR stands as an innovative beacon of hope, offering a captivating, hands-on approach to the exploration of the cosmos.

6.1. VR and Experiential Learning

The traditional chalk-and-talk method of teaching science is making way for experiential, learn-by-doing methods. The term "experiential learning" stems from educational theorist David Kolb's concept implying that optimal learning is a process that focuses on gaining knowledge and skills from direct experience, not merely from reading texts or listening to lectures.

VR, in this respect, is a leap forward in experiential learning. It brings to life the vastness and intricacy of the universe in ways unimaginable with conventional methods. By leveraging VR, educators can transform classrooms into space laboratories, leading students through the adventure of exploring galaxies and planets from the convenience of their school desks.

6.2. Interactive Journey through the Universe

VR technology enables learners to take a step beyond classroom constraints and immerse themselves in realistic depictions of the cosmos. Donning the headset, they can journey through space, visit celestial bodies, and observe them up close. This experience motivates deeper understanding, promotes concept retention, and cultivates the intellectual curiosity imperative for scientific studies.

What sets VR apart is its ability to make vast distances and scales intuitive. For instance, trying to make sense of the massive scale of our Milky Way Galaxy from a textbook or even a video can be daunting. Alternatively, an interactive VR journey offers a tangible comprehension of the enormous distances between galaxies and the relative sizes of different celestial bodies.

6.3. Emphasizing Systems Over Isolated Facts

One of the key strengths of employing VR in education is its capacity to illustrate the interconnectedness of various components and systems. In the context of astrophysics, this includes showcasing the relationships between planets, stars, galaxies, and other celestial systems. Understanding these intricate relationships often becomes easier and more intuitive when they are experienced dynamically in VR environments.

It is indeed challenging to teach students about the force of gravity, the rotation and revolution of planets, or the lifecycle of stars, relying solely on two-dimensional diagrams and descriptions. Implementing VR circumvents these constraints, creating extraordinarily real and interactive renditions of these sophisticated phenomena.

6.4. Virtual Lab Experiments

The potential of VR isn't limited to guiding students through space. It can be utilized to perform virtual lab experiments that mirror the complexities of a real-world physics lab. In a VR lab, students can experiment with variables such as gravity and light and observe their effects firsthand without risks associated with real-world experiments.

Virtual labs provide a safe space for learners to make mistakes, test hypotheses, and learn from interactive experimentation. Consequently, they help build problem-solving skills, step away from rote learning, and encourage the application of theory in practice.

6.5. Transcending Accessibility Barriers

The immersive nature of VR transcends geographical barriers, offering students everywhere equal access to hands-on astrophysics learning. By emulating trips to space or scientific labs, VR eliminates logistical impossibilities, making education in astrophysics inclusive and global. This democratization of education is particularly relevant in regions where astronomy and physics materials might be sparse or non-existent.

6.6. Future of VR in Astrophysics Education

Bearing the potential to transform the educational landscape, the future of VR in astrophysics education is highly promising. The scalability and adaptability of VR make it a versatile tool capable of evolving with advancements in astrophysics and educational pedagogies.

The prospect of creating more engaging, tailored learning environments through AI and adaptive learning techniques also buttress the promise of VR. These advancements could help tailor education to individual students, continually adapting to fit their needs.

In conclusion, the integration of VR in astrophysics offers a transformative approach to learning that underpins the principles of experiential learning, promotes the assimilation of complex concepts, and fosters an environment of interactive comprehension and curiosity. This blend of advanced learning and technology brings us closer than ever to the cosmos, fueling the growing attraction towards astrophysics and facilitating the intrepid, scholarly exploration of our infinite universe.

Chapter 7. Astro-tourism: Harnessing VR for Virtual Space Exploration

In an age where physical boundaries often limit our desire for exploration, Virtual Reality (VR) emerges as an extraordinary tool, enabling us to traverse previously inaccessible realms. One such domain is our vast and awe-inspiring universe, a fascination that's gripped mankind since the dawn of civilization. As we harness VR for space exploration, we're not merely viewing celestial bodies from afar, but embarking on a first-person, immersive journey to witness their majesty incredibly close.

7.1. Breaking the Bonds of Earth

The beauty of VR lies in its ability to offer an immersive experience, unbounded by physical realities. Traditional stargazing usually requires equipment like telescopes, and clear, pollution-free skies. Even then, you're limited to a narrow, two-dimensional view of the heavenly expanse. On the other hand, VR surpasses these limitations, enabling users to virtually voyage to the outermost reaches of the cosmos, almost making the observers feel like they might be stepping on distant planets or hovering in close proximity to stars.

Astrophysical simulations and models provide the foundation for these VR experiences. They convert complex datasets into visual spectacles, enabling us to observe cosmic phenomena that often span millennia within a comfortable time frame. This acts as a significant educational tool for disseminating astrophysics knowledge to a broader audience.

7.2. Journey to the Stars

Coupled with VR headsets and guided by scientifically accurate data, you're able to embark on journeys to distant celestial bodies – sidereal trips that human bodies aren't structurally or genetically equipped to undertake. Imagine navigating the rugged terrain of Mars, touring our own lunar surface, capturing a close-up view of the stormy surface of Jupiter, or even coasting through the vibrant, multicolored writhes of a nebula. The possibilities are bound only by our current knowledge of space.

Much of the information for these visualizations is gleaned from space probes and telescopes, like the Hubble Telescope. These observatories and probes offer a vast treasure trove of high-definition views, capturing the authentic colors, movements, and structures of outer space phenomena. When integrated into VR environments, they make space tourism an incredible, breathtaking experience.

7.3. The Virtual Astronaut Experience

The thrill of being an astronaut, experiencing zero gravity, and viewing Earth from a space capsule are now within reach for everyone thanks to VR technology. Various space agencies, like NASA, and private corporations like SpaceX are investing in VR to offer immersive astronaut training simulations, both for their astronauts and the general public.

However, it's not just about uplifting off into outer space without leaving your home. It's also about experiencing the day-to-day life on the International Space Station (ISS), performing space walks, engaging in satellite repair, and witnessing the grandeur of our planet from above. It's an experience that is sure to provoke a sense of wonder and appreciation for the grand scale of the universe and our place within it.

7.4. Education and Outreach

For educators and astronomy outreach programs, VR offers unprecedented pedagogical opportunities. It's one thing to read about the stars or watch a documentary. It's quite another to virtually fly to a distant galaxy. Equipped with VR, educators can take students on an interactive tour of the universe, answering questions, explaining phenomena, and kindling their curiosity. VR can serve as the planetarium of the future, engaging students in experiential learning, thereby fostering better comprehension and retention.

7.5. Future Perspectives: From Virtual to Actual

The advent of VR in astrophysics isn't just revolutionizing how we observe and learn about the cosmos; it's also redefining the future of space exploration. VR could become a preliminary tool for actual space exploration, with rovers and spacecrafts first virtually mapping out our universe. By doing so, they could identify potential points of interest or sites for landings and resource collection, and predict and plan for unexpected situations, paving the way for safer, more efficient human space exploration.

In conclusion, the fusion of VR with astrophysics is creating an ocean of possibilities for virtual space exploration, also known as astro-tourism. It transcends traditional experience bounds, offering an immersive, detailed exploration of our cosmos. As we look ahead, we envisage astro-tourism being a major part of space studies, contributing to the democratization of space exploration and building a more cosmic-aware society. For now, sit back, strap on your VR headset, and prepare for a journey where no one has gone before. The universe is waiting!

Chapter 8. Hands on the Cosmos: Advancements in VR and Astrophysical Interactivity

The fusion of virtual reality (VR) technology and astrophysics has triggered a powerful wave of innovation that's reinventing our interaction with the cosmos. This revolutionary amalgamation gives individuals the capability to observe, analyse, and learn about celestial bodies with unprecedented immersiveness, ultimately progressing the way we understand our universe.

8.1. Virtual Immersion into the Cosmos

Virtual reality, with its immersive capabilities, allows us to convert raw astronomical data into interactive 3D experiences. State-of-the-art VR headsets like the Oculus Rift and the HTC Vive have transformed computer screens into immersive stargazing platforms, providing an unparalleled perception of the cosmos.

NASA, for example, utilized the power of VR to curate an interactive journey through the microscopic world of the International Space Station (ISS). This technology enriches astronomical learning experiences, letting individuals explore complex spatial relationships and witness cosmic phenomenons from a whole new viewpoint.

8.2. Data Visualization in Astrophysics

Data visualization plays an integral role in astrophysics. Data from telescopes, particularly those like the Hubble Space, the Chandra X-ray Observatory, and the Keck Observatory, produce copious amounts of data which is critical to understanding the universe. However, interpreting this data can be an arduous task due to its complex and abstract nature.

VR technology combats this issue by facilitating the transformation of raw data into comprehensive 3D models, allowing for easy manipulation and better understanding - a feat not possible through traditional tech interfaces. Whether sifting through the cosmic microwave background radiation or mapping galaxy distributions, this incredible feature propels both learning and discovery in astrophysics.

8.3. Virtual Laboratories and Simulations

One of the most invaluable applications of VR in astrophysics is the establishment of virtual labs and simulations. Through gaming engines like Unity and Unreal Engine, developers have created realistic simulations that accurately portray cosmic events.

These reliable and repeatable environments provide tools to experiment with variables, break and rebuild constructs, ultimately offering precious insights that would typically require expensive physical resources or lengthy observational periods. VR simulations provide a unique sandbox, where theoretical models can be tested and observed in real-time, tightening the loop between theory, observation, and understanding.

8.4. Deepening Public Engagement

Perhaps the most exciting aspect of this breakthrough is how it invites the general public to engage with the universe in an intimate way. With numerous apps and programs available, anyone with a VR headset can immerse themselves in the cosmos, experiencing stellar phenomena that were only accessible to astrophysicists and astronomers before.

Google's Tilt Brush VR application, for instance, enables users to express their creativity by drawing and exploring in 3D spaces. These kind of applications make astronomy more engaging for students, stirring up their interest in science, technology, engineering, and mathematics (STEM) fields.

8.5. Conclusion

To the dedicated astrophysicist, VR is an invaluable tool that equips them with a heightened perception of the universe. To the curious novice, VR is the spaceship, the magic carpet that whisks them away on thrilling journeys across cosmic landscapes.

As technological advancements accelerate, the potential for exploration into the cosmos continues to broaden. VR is at the core of this, enabling science to convert vast quantities of abstract data into tangible experiences, pushing the way we perceive and understand the universe. It's not an exaggeration to say that these remarkable advancements in VR and astrophysical interactivity are, quite literally, enabling us to grasp the cosmos in our hands.

Chapter 9. Case Studies: Significant Contributions of VR in Astrophysical Discoveries

Ever since the advent of virtual reality (VR), the cosmos has seemed less distant. Astounding technologies converge, allowing us to explore distant galaxies and interact with celestial bodies from the comfort of our homes. Here we explore several notable instances where VR has contributed significantly to astrophysical discoveries.

===VR as an Analytical Tool

VR is not just a medium for delivering content – it is becoming increasingly clear that it can serve as a powerful tool for analysis in astrophysics. When the Event Horizon Telescope (EHT) captured the first image of a black hole in 2019, VR played a considerable role in interpreting the unprecedented data.

The image was challenging to process given it was gathered from a network of eight telescopes positioned worldwide. However, by integrating the data into a VR environment, astrophysicists could visualize the black hole's event horizon in three dimensions, providing a more intuitive understanding.

===Exploring the Cosmos: The Mars Rover Experience

The Mars Rover is an exceptional case of VR's contributions to space exploration. NASA uses VR to maneuver the Rover remotely, recreating a Martian environment that engineers can navigate to plan the Rover's next moves. This application of VR technology has been instrumental in multiple successful Mars missions, enhancing our understanding of the Red Planet's surface and atmospheric conditions.

Furthermore, this VR technology has been adapted into an educational experience made available to the public. This inspirational educational tool offers anyone with a headset the opportunity to virtually traipse across Martian soil, revealing just how VR can not only serve scientific discovery but also cultivate public interest and engagement.

===Seeing Through the Clouds: The Titan Saturn System Mission

NASA's upcoming Titan Saturn System Mission (Dragonfly) exemplifies how VR can enable the exploration of distant celestial bodies. The Dragonfly mission aims to send a drone to Saturn's moon, Titan, exploring its surface and atmosphere.

Given the dense, clouded atmosphere of Titan, conventional photography and video are inadequate for exploration. However, an onboard camera will capture VR imagery and terrain information, enabling scientists back on Earth to navigate the drone and investigate intriguing features virtually.

===Gravitational Waves and VR

The Laser Interferometer Gravitational-Wave Observatory (LIGO) made headlines in 2016 when it detected gravitational waves for the first time. Beyond this achievement, LIGO has harnessed VR technology to enhance data interpretation.

LIGO's VR application translates the detected gravitational waves into visual and auditory experiences. This approach not only provides a valuable method for exploring complex data but also makes the concept of gravitational waves accessible to a broader audience, emphasizing VR's potential as an educational tool in addition to research.

===Simulating Galaxy Formation

One of the most extensive implementations of VR in astrophysics has been in simulating galaxy formation. The galaxies we observe today were formed over billions of years, involving complex processes and influences that are impossible to observe directly.

Using data from the Hubble Space Telescope and infra-red telescopic surveys, scientists have developed detailed simulations that outline potential paths of galaxy evolution. These simulations, when integrated with VR, allow scientists to observe the life cycle of galaxies, gaining crucial insights about our universe's structure and history.

As can be seen from these cases, VR proves itself as a powerful tool in astrophysical discoveries, enabling scientists to visualize and navigate astronomical data remarkably. It becomes increasingly apparent that the future of exploring our universe will incorporate immersive technologies like VR. As we continue to embrace this tool and refine its applications, not even the sky will be the limit for our cosmic curiosities.

Chapter 10. Future Scope: Predictions and Innovations in VR-Enabled Astrophysics

From the perspective of astrophysics, the advent of Virtual Reality (VR) has opened up whole new avenues for exploration and learning. By immersing us in simulations of the universe, VR offers firsthand encounters with celestial bodies and galaxies light-years away, augmenting the way we understand and interact with space. As we look ahead, potentials of this technology in the field of astrophysics seem boundless.

10.1. Emphasizing Immersive Learning

When it comes to studying and understanding the complexity of the universe, immersive learning brought about by VR proves to be a game-changer. It affords learners an opportunity to interactively immerse themselves in the celestial arena, observing and manipulating celestial bodies at different scales – facilitating a kinesthetic learning approach otherwise impossible.

Future iterations of such systems will likely offer higher immersion levels, enhancing spatial, auditory, and even haptic feedback. Advances in wearable tech such as haptic gloves and VR treadmills will provide a more realistic 'feel' of space. Imagine feeling the weightlessness of space right from your living room, or studying the surface of Mars, experience its rocky texture, and understanding the sheer magnitude of Olympus Mons, the largest volcano in our solar system.

10.2. Revolutionizing Data Visualization

VR opens up new horizons in visualizing astronomical data. The ability to convert 2D data into 3D representations can revolutionize our understanding of space phenomena. Researchers are already using VR to analyze patterns in cosmic microwave background radiation or to visualize intricate structures of galaxies.

In terms of future scope, VR could play a pivotal role in visualizing and understanding complex multivariate data sets in astrophysics. A time may come when astrophysicists would explore intricate multi-dimensional datasets and gain insights into cosmic mysteries such as dark matter and dark energy, all within VR-created universes.

10.3. Enabling Interstellar Exploration

Technological advancements in VR could allow astrophysicists to 'explore' distant galaxies and even black holes, interactions with which are currently limited to data received by telescopes or space probes. Through VR, scientists could simulate environments around these cosmic wonders, offering novel perspectives that can push the boundaries of human knowledge about the cosmos.

This technology could also bolster the planning and execution of interstellar missions. Mars rovers and other robotic explorers of the future could be steered from Earth using VR, providing astronauts or researchers with a first-person perspective and tactile feedback, thereby increasing mission success rates.

10.4. Enhancing Public Outreach

As VR becomes more affordable and widespread, it could serve as a revolutionary tool for public outreach in astrophysics. Schools and science centers could make astronomy more engaging and inclusive by conducting virtual field trips to Mars, or simulating a walk on the moon.

Moreover, future developments could lead to home-based VR astronomy systems that could bring stargazing concerts into people's living rooms. A day may arrive when, instead of simply looking at images of Hubble's discoveries, one can journey through the nebulae and star fields themselves.

10.5. Fostering International Collaboration

In the realm of scientific research, VR can play a major role in fostering international collaboration. VR enables scientists from around the world to interact with the same set of data, in real time, making it a potent tool for global scientific discourse.

By embracing VR, astrophysicists across the globe can collaborate on monumental explorations of cosmic mysteries, reducing geographical limitations and enabling the pooling of intellectual resources.

10.6. Conclusion: Towards the Future

The potential for VR in astrophysics is indeed intriguing. As this technology advances, it carries the promise of unmatched learning, improved data visualization, enhanced exploration, wider public outreach, and international collaboration.

While there are barriers to overcome, such as improving technology validity and reducing cost, there is no denying the transformative capacity of VR. The day when we will be able to virtually travel through the universe, witnessing cosmic events and studying celestial bodies firsthand, might indeed be closer than we think. The continuous heartbeat of human innovation is pushing us forward into this grand VR-enabled era of astrophysics.

Chapter 11. Beyond the Frontiers of Space: The Ultimate Guide to Getting Started with VR in Astrophysics

With Virtual Reality (VR), the wide, endless expanse of the cosmos isn't as unreachable as it once seemed. This technology allows us to speedily traverse the grandeur of space from the comfort of our living rooms. It's an exciting frontier for both space exploration and education – a mixture of the real and the virtual, melding two seemingly disparate fields into one comprehensive, immersive experience. Through this thrilling synthesis, we can finally journey beyond our Earthly boundaries without ever actually leaving solid ground.

Before we embark on this Universe-spanning odyssey, it's important to build a fundamental understanding of VR and how it ties into astrophysics.

11.1. VR: A Primer

Virtual reality is a computer-generated simulation of a three-dimensional environment. Users interact within this environment using special electronic equipment such as a helmet with a screen or gloves fitted with sensors. In essence, it offers simulated experiences that can be similar to or completely different from the real world. The robust immersive environment that VR provides is what makes it an attractive choice for a myriad of applications, from gaming to training, architecture, and now, astrophysics.

The major components of a typical VR setup include a Head Mounted Display (HMD), tracking system, and input devices. HMD is a visual display unit you wear on your head like a helmet, which effectively blocks out all ambient light, immerses you in the virtual world, and tracks your head movements. The tracking system monitors your position and orientation so the rendered environment changes accordingly. Input devices, such as controllers, gloves, or voice recognition software, allow you to interact with the virtual world.

11.2. VR and Astrophysics

Astrophysics, a branch of astronomy that deals with the physical nature and dynamic processes of celestial objects and phenomena, has long struggled to make its complex subtleties easily understandable. Dense with mind-bending concepts and mathematical abstraction, the field can be daunting for beginners and the uninitiated.

Enter VR and its potential to fundamentally change the way we learn and understand astrophysics. By offering a simulated, exploratory environment that's experiential rather than purely theoretical, VR gives us a 'hands-on' experience of space elements and physical laws. You can, for example, manipulate galaxies with your own hands or dive into a black hole to witness the singularity - concepts otherwise difficult to wrap your head around.

Coupled with sensorial feedback, VR provides an unmatched perspective of the cosmos that goes beyond looking at 2D textbooks or 3D planetarium shows.

11.3. Setting Up Your VR

To get started with VR in astrophysics, you will first need to invest in a VR device. Some of the popular options include Oculus Rift, HTC Vive, or Sony's PlayStation VR. These systems can vary significantly regarding price and hardware requirements, so you should choose according to your budget and the kind of computer system you already have.

Download the VR astrophysics application of your choice on your computer and connect your VR device. Some of the popular ones include:

- Titans of Space – provides a grand tour of our Solar System and a few stars in nearby interstellar space.

- Universe Sandbox – lets you control the laws of nature to change the universe on a cosmic scale.

- Space Walk VR Experience – allows a visually enchanting walk on the International Space Station.

When everything is set up, wear your VR helmet, and make sure your movement space is clear of obstructions. Start the application and immerse yourself fully. You will see a calibration screen asking you to adjust the position of your VR helmet and possibly the controllers. Follow the on-screen instructions, and you're good to go.

11.4. Navigating the Cosmos

In almost all VR experiences, you'll have the ability to 'teleport'. Simply point your controller to where you want to go and press the appropriate button. Some simulations allow you to 'fly' through space, giving a natural, immersive experience of floating amidst stars, planets, and galaxies. This not only gives the user a chance to examine celestial objects up close but also a sense of scale that is difficult to get from a textbook.

11.5. Conclusion

This is just the beginning. As advancements in VR technology continue, we'll be able to enjoy more nuanced and enriched explorations into the cosmic realm, stimulating an even higher degree of immersion and offering a more in-depth understanding of the Universe around us.

Getting started with VR in astrophysics is not as daunting as you might think, and the potential reward is a tour that takes you, albeit virtually, all the way to the edge of the Universe and beyond. Armed with your VR headset and controller, the confines of our universe are the only limits.

So go ahead, don your Virtual reality headset and brace yourself for a cosmic journey unlike any before. Points of light will become distinct planets, stars will grow to enormous proportions, and you'll lose yourself amongst the very cosmos themselves. It's high time we pushed the frontiers of space exploration, and VR in astrophysics lets us do exactly that.